E   BOOK OF

PARTY
GAMES

• The Essential Guide to Grown-up Fun •

RUTH CULLEN

ILLUSTRATED BY KERREN BARBAS

 PETER PAUPER PRESS, INC.
WHITE PLAINS, NEW YORK

FOR JAY,
WHO REALLY KNOWS
HOW TO PARTY

Designed by Heather Zschock
Illustrations copyright © 2006 Kerren Barbas

Copyright © 2006
Peter Pauper Press, Inc.
202 Mamaroneck Avenue
White Plains, NY 10601
All rights reserved
ISBN 1-59359-919-6
Printed in Hong Kong
7 6 5 4 3 2 1

Visit us at www.peterpauper.com

Peter Pauper Press, Inc. and the author have used their best efforts to ensure that the directions for each drinking game are correct. We urge readers to use their discretion and good sense in playing these games, and not to do anything ill-advised. Ultimately, responsible drinking is everyone's personal responsibility.

THE LITTLE
BLACK BOOK OF

PARTY
GAMES

CONTENTS

INTRODUCTION

When is the last time you went to a *great* party? Not just an *OK* party. Not *better-than-reruns*. We're talking *fun! Stimulating! Entertaining!* The kind of party you just can't stop thinking about—and not because of your pounding hangover.

Was it the food? The music? The location? Or was it something else?

Before you throw yet another boring party where people loiter by the hors d'oeuvres table and talk about the weather, ask yourself a few simple questions:

- *How will I make my guests feel comfortable and at ease from the moment they arrive?*
- *What can I do to get people talking?*
- *How do I make my party memorable for each one of my guests?*

The answer lies right in your hot little hands. PARTY GAMES!

Party games go way beyond the *Musical Chairs* and *Pin-the-Tail-on-the-Donkey* of your youth, and they are certainly not just for children. Looking for a way to introduce your friends and acquaintances? Try an icebreaker! Want to crank up the heat? Play a naughty game!

In *The Little Black Book of Party Games*, you will find all sorts of possibilities that are sure to make your next big bash the talk of the town—for all the right reasons.

Say goodbye to those awkward moments in front of the punch bowl, and hello to good, clean fun. Got games?

let's get
this party started

Spring is nature's way of saying,
"Let's party!"

ROBIN WILLIAMS

Dust off the lamp shades and stock up the fridge—it's party time! You don't need a reason or a grand master plan. And you certainly don't need an ice sculpture. What you do need is a certain *joie de vivre*—a zest for life. A spirit of fun.

It is in this spirit that you should plan your party, paying special attention to four main areas: *people, place, refreshments, and games.*

PEOPLE

People make parties. No matter how delicious the hummus or gorgeous the setting, a party isn't a party without the *people*.

When assembling your guest list, choose an eclectic group of individuals with as many differences as similarities. It's as easy as making a Waldorf salad—some fruit, some veggies, and a few nuts. This marriage of opposites makes for engaging conversation and is sure to spark a lively party dynamic.

Of course, some guest lists come ready-made and are inherently unbalanced, such as those for certain family gatherings or business-related functions. For these situations and party planning in general, always think specifically of your guests, and plan the details with them in mind.

PLACE

Wallflowers need walls just as couch potatoes need couches. But above all, your party guests need to feel comfortable at your party—whether it's in your living room, outside by the pool, or in a banquet hall. Your guests will appreciate your attention to the small but important details that might otherwise put a damper on festivities.

Is the location you've selected for your party convenient for your guests? Do you have ample seating and standing areas? Are bathrooms accessible and well-stocked? Are parking areas nearby and clearly marked? Will the location of food and drink stations facilitate the traffic flow of your guests?

Working out your party's logistics ahead of time shows your guests you care, and, better yet, frees you to party with them once they arrive.

REFRESHMENTS

Nothing says, "Let's party" like a bowl of rum punch and a table of hors d'oeuvres. Parties mean trays of lasagna and pigs in blankets, crudités and artichoke dip. Drinks flow like water, loosening tongues and stirring up the fun. And when champagne corks fly, that can mean only one thing: cake. You simply can't have a party without some form of cake.

At your party, don't skimp on the refreshments. Too much may leave you with leftovers, but not enough will send your guests packing. That said, too much of the wrong thing (e.g., nuts, sugary or fatty foods) can send your guests packing their hospital bags if

they suffer from food allergies or specific medical conditions.

These days, as a courtesy and a precaution, you should ask your guests if they have any special dietary needs. While you need not plan your food and drink menus totally around the exceptions, these folks will think that *you* are exceptional for thinking of them and providing them some alternatives.

GAMES

Socializing does not come easily to everyone. Some people view the prospect of making conversation with strangers to be downright terrifying, while others find themselves at a loss for words without the security blanket of cell phones and handheld computers.

Party games serve as a social lubricant—easing people into conversation and helping them make the connection with others. And these days, despite all of our technological connections, people feel more disconnected than ever. They yearn to socialize—to practice the lost art of making conversation outside the context of work or family.

As host, make it your mission to facilitate this connection among your guests.

The right game at the right time can bridge the gap between people and help them reveal different sides of themselves. And once they do, your party will take on a life of its own.

*Life is like a game of cards.
The hand you are dealt is
determinism; the way you
play it is free will.*

JAWAHARLAL NEHRU

how game are you?

*I am thankful for the mess to clean
after a party because it means
I have been surrounded by friends.*

Nancie J. Carmody

It's your party, and you can play whatever games you want, right?

Right. But if you want your guests to join in the fun, consider their perspectives while deciding what games to play and when to play them. And throwing in a few incentives never hurts, either.

WHAT TO PLAY

In deciding what games to play, consider the type of party you're throwing and the personalities of the guests you've invited.

Big outdoor parties are naturals for physical games involving balls and props, unless the age, physical ability, or dress of your guests prevents them from participating. Small indoor gatherings set the stage for interactive group activities and games that don't require much physical movement.

But beware: not everyone in your captive audience may be "game" to playing games, especially if they involve excessive drinking, revealing too-personal information, or acting silly.

It's up to you as host to gauge how receptive your guests will be to different types of games, and choose accordingly. Of course, you should not pressure people to do something they don't want to do, or otherwise make them feel like party poopers.

Just keep a laser-like focus on your mission—*FUN*—and whatever you choose will be the right choice.

WHEN TO PLAY

So much of your party's success depends on timing. Knowing when to introduce games can be the deciding factor in whether or not they succeed.

With the exception of certain icebreakers or "meet and greet" activities, allow your guests some time to get a feel for their surroundings. Make introductions, offer food and drink, and give them an opportunity to socialize and mingle.

At the *right* time—that is, whenever you sense a lull in your party's momentum or any profound exuberance of your guests—intro-

duce a game. If you're lucky, one game will lead to the next, getting progressively more festive each time.

If your game flops, or your guests clearly prefer

the bowl of chips to the game of charades, then let them munch. When they're ready, try again with something else that you believe will enhance your party and appeal to your guests.

PRIZES AND AWARDS

Just the remote possibility of winning a prize sells millions of lottery tickets every day. People love to test their luck and skill, and feel great satisfaction when they unearth that plastic toy from the box of cereal, or score the big win at the local carnival and claim the oversized, neon-colored stuffed animal.

You don't have to tempt your party crowd with prizes and awards in order for them to have fun, but when you do, everyone wins.

Your guests will jump into the action the moment they know a prize is at stake, regardless of its value. Hit the discount store to find a potpourri of choices—candles, kitchen gadgets, gardening tools—or make it interesting with gourmet coffee beans, lottery or movie tickets, or bottles of wine. Gag gifts keep things lighthearted and can be hilarious, as can creative awards such as "Best Bluffer" or "Most Misunderstood."

Only you will know what types of carrots to dangle before your party guests, but the carrots themselves are not quite as important as the role they serve—to get your party hopping!

let the
games begin

*The goal of all civilization, all
religious thought, and all that sort of
thing is simply to have a good time.*

Don Marquis

The games that follow are grouped into seven main categories: *Icebreakers; Word Games; Physical Games; Silly Games; Mystery Games; Drinking Games; and Naughty Games.*

Within each category, you will find all the information you need about each game and its variations (if any), with clear instructions on how to play. Pertinent "tips" will keep you on track and moving in the right direction.

But before you break out the score pad, there are a few more (sometimes sticky) details to consider, such as how to organize players into pairs or teams. And what about those ultra-competitive types who spoil everyone else's fun?

How to Organize Players

 It's very important to exercise caution when choosing teams or pairing up guests for your next party game, lest you recreate someone's junior high school nightmare. No one likes to be chosen last or by default in any game, whether it's *Pictionary* or dodge ball.

Here are some easy time-tested ways to organize players.

Choosing "It":

Ask for a Volunteer:
An easy and usually successful option, depending on the game.

Draw Straws/Pencils/Sticks:
Everyone picks one straw/pencil/stick of

varied length from a bunch, and whoever draws the shortest straw/pencil/stick is "It."

LOTTERY:

Everyone draws a folded slip of paper from a bowl in which one paper contains an "X." Whoever picks the "X" is "It."

Forming Pairs and Teams:

COUPLE SHUFFLE:

Randomly rearrange married couples or close friends into pairs.

LOTTERY FOR PAIRS:

Everyone draws a folded slip of paper from a bowl in which pairs of paper have the same markings (e.g., blue dots, red triangles, etc.). Players with matching papers form pairs.

LOTTERY FOR TEAMS:

Everyone draws a folded slip of paper from a bowl in which half the papers contain an "X." The X's form one team, the blank papers another.

COMPETITION AND GAMESMANSHIP

Games bring out the best in us—and sometimes the worst.

Faster than you can say, "Cha ching! I win again!" an ominous cloud can form above your game table, growing larger and larger with each huffy breath from . . . *the competitor*.

The competitor simply can't "compete" for fun. He rears his ugly head in casual games of Scrabble and lighthearted rounds of croquet, playing to win, and winning at all costs—even if it means bending the rules or sabotaging the efforts of others. Don't let

any such competitors spoil your party by transforming your friendly game into an Olympic event.

As host, you've got the referee's whistle, so blow it and say, "You. Penalty box. Now!" Or, you can just call a timeout and re-direct your guests to other activities, such as eating and drinking.

If you wish, use this opportunity to confront the offender ("David, you are hereby cut off from *Scrabble* until you can play nicely with the other boys and girls."), or have a drink yourself and let the whole episode slide. It's a party, after all.

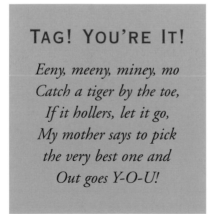

TAG! YOU'RE IT!

Eeny, meeny, miney, mo
Catch a tiger by the toe,
If it hollers, let it go,
My mother says to pick
the very best one and
Out goes Y-O-U!

the games

*Someone said that life is a party.
You join in after it's started and
leave before it's finished.*

ELSA MAXWELL

Icebreakers

Icebreakers are welcoming games intended to relax guests and facilitate introductions and conversation. Consider using icebreakers at parties or social gatherings with lots of casual acquaintances or brand new faces, or any time you wish to get to know your guests a little better.

Cocktail party: A gathering held to enable forty people to talk about themselves at the same time.

FRED ALLEN

WHO AM I?

(a.k.a. Famous Names, Famous Characters)

OBJECTIVE:

To guess the name on your back by obtaining clues from other guests.

NUMBER OF PLAYERS: 5+

MATERIALS NEEDED:
- Adhesive nametags for each guest
- Pen or marker

SUMMARY:

The host places a nametag with a famous name on the back of each player. (See page 34 for ideas.) Players ask other guests one "yes or no" question at a time in an attempt to figure out the names on their own backs.

HOW TO PLAY:

1. Before the party, the host fills out nametags with the names of famous people (e.g., William Shakespeare, Oprah

Winfrey), making sure there are enough for each guest.

2. As guests arrive, the host places nametags containing famous names on their backs, being careful that they do not see their own nametags. Guests may ask only one "yes or no" question at a time of each guest to figure out their identity, and must then move on to another guest to ask a question. For example: *Am I living? Am I deceased? Am I a woman? Have I served in political office?*

3. Guests circulate throughout the party, obtaining as many clues as necessary. When they think they know who they are, they approach the host and say, "Am I (name of person)?" If incorrect, they continue asking questions of other guests until they get it right or give up. The first

guest to correctly identify himself or herself wins!

Ideas for Famous Names:

Movie Stars	*Cartoon*
Politicians	*Characters*
Professional	*Singers*
Athletes	*News Anchors*
Famous Authors	*Comedians*

VARIATIONS:

1. Instead of people, choose names of anything at all (e.g., countries, sea creatures, flowers, Chinese food entrées, condiments), or names of particular interest to the group. For example, if you're throwing a toga party, choose mythical gods and characters as your list of names to choose from.

2. You can also play this game by acting like a famous person, and having other guests try to figure out your identity.

Cover your mirrors! Also, if you don't know your guests very well, or your guests don't know each other, select famous names or things that can be relatively easy to guess.

The popular game Chutes and Ladders *can be traced to the game* Snakes and Ladders, *originally an Indian game used in religious instruction, and later modified by the Victorians to reinforce their moral ideals. Nineteenth-century English virtues would elevate a player up a ladder, while vices would slide a player down.*

JOVIAL PURSUIT

Great way for friends and casual acquaintances to learn more about each other!

OBJECTIVE:
To match guest trivia with the correct person.

NUMBER OF PLAYERS: 5–30

MATERIALS NEEDED:
- Guest trivia, collected before party
- Adhesive nametags

SUMMARY:
Guests try to match trivia with the person to whom it applies by asking questions of other guests. When they correctly match the triv-ia with the person, they shout, "Match!" and place the trivia nametag on the guest to wear for the rest of the party.

HOW TO PLAY:

1. At some point before the party, the host solicits two key pieces of trivia information from each guest: one unique or surprising fact about them, and their favorite hobby. (See page 38 for additional trivia ideas.) The host then writes this information on adhesive nametags, one for each guest.

2. When party guests arrive, the host gives them a nametag containing another guest's trivia, and instructs them to try to match the trivia with the guest. They should circulate the room and ask pointed questions of other guests related to the information on the nametag (e.g., "Were you ever in a rock band called *The Renegade Frogs?*").

Additional Trivia Ideas	
First Job/Car	*Dream Job*
Birthplace	*Favorite*
Favorite Book/	*Song/Food/*
Movie/TV Show	*Vacation Spot*
College Major	

3. When a guest finds a match (e.g., "Yeah! Are you an old *Frogs* fan? Oh, it's on the tag."), he shouts, "Match!" and places a trivia nametag on the guest to wear for the rest of the party.

VARIATIONS:

1. The host compiles trivia information onto one sheet of paper, and distributes copies to guests when they arrive. Guests  attempt to match trivia with other guests as they circulate throughout the party. The first guest to correctly match up all the trivia correctly wins a prize.

Correct answers are read aloud for the benefit of the group.

2. See Icebreaker Bingo on page 45.

2. See Icebreaker Bingo on page 45.

TIP:

Don't get too personal with trivia questions (e.g., age, years of marriage, number of children). Choose subjects that will reveal hints about people's personalities and make for fun conversation starters.

GENIUS

Perfect activity and conversation starter for large groups of people!

OBJECTIVE:
To guess the correct (or most nearly correct) answers to a series of problems or scenarios.

NUMBER OF PLAYERS: 6+

MATERIALS NEEDED:
- A glass jar containing M&Ms, dried beans, or peanuts (counted)
- A large book, such as a dictionary or textbook
- A photograph of a child
- A shoe
- A food item, price tag removed (e.g., box of cereal, can of tuna)
- Paper and pencil for each player

SUMMARY:

A guessing game in which guests visit stations set up throughout the party and record their best guesses to a series of problems or scenarios.

HOW TO PLAY:

1. Before the party, the host sets up stations in different locations throughout the party featuring the following: a glass jar filled with M&Ms; a dictionary; a photograph of a child; a shoe; and a box of cereal. At each station, the host places a piece of paper and the following questions:

   - *How many M&Ms are in the jar?*
   - *How many pages are in the book?*
   - *How old is the child in the photograph?*
   - *How much does the shoe weigh?*
   - *How much did the box of cereal cost?*

2. When guests arrive, the host gives them paper and pencils, and advises them to visit the different guessing games stationed

throughout the party and record their guesses.

3. At a designated time, the host collects the players' guesses, announces the correct answers, and recognizes the winner (Genius!) with a prize.

VARIATION:

You may vary the challenges in this game to include anything you wish—the height of a candle, the width of a picture frame, the volume of liquid in a vase. The goal is to bring people together while they hypothesize about different scenarios, and get them circulating throughout the party.

TIP:

Don't turn off your guests by making the problems too difficult or obscure. People should feel reasonably confident about their guesses—or at least in the ballpark.

AUTOGRAPH

Great way to facilitate introductions!

OBJECTIVE:

To be the first person to collect autographs from all party guests.

NUMBER OF PLAYERS: 8+

MATERIALS NEEDED:

- Party guest lists, typed or hand-written, for each guest
- Pens or pencils for each guest

SUMMARY:

Guests mix and mingle in an attempt to be the first person to collect signatures from everyone at the party.

HOW TO PLAY:

1. Before the party, the host makes copies of the guest list, enough for each guest.

2. When guests arrive, they are each provided a copy of the guest list and a pen, and advised that the first person to collect autographs from everyone at the party will win a prize.

3. Guests socialize and mingle, and the first person to present the host with a completely signed guest list is the official winner.

TIP:

Try this game with groups of strangers or casual acquaintances.

ICEBREAKER BINGO

Perfect for parties with lots of new faces!

OBJECTIVE:

To facilitate conversation and help guests get to know each other.

NUMBER OF PLAYERS: 6–30

MATERIALS NEEDED:

- Bingo cards for all players, prepared in advance
- Pens or pencils for each guest

SUMMARY:

Party guests socialize with other guests in an effort to gather information needed to complete bingo cards. The first player to complete his bingo card wins!

HOW TO PLAY:

1. Before the party, the host creates bingo cards in which each square contains a

fact about one of the party guests. For example, squares might read, "scratch golfer" or "fluent in six languages." Bingo cards can be tailored to accommodate all the guests at the party.

2. When guests arrive, they receive bingo cards and writing utensils and are instructed to talk to other guests in order to gather information and cross off squares on their bingo cards. The first person to cross off all the squares on their bingo card wins!

TIP:

For larger parties, include some information on bingo cards that can apply to more than one guest (e.g., "drives a minivan," "tells great jokes").

SNAPSHOT

An instant conversation starter and creative means of self expression!

OBJECTIVE:

To help guests get to know each other in a fun and non-threatening way.

NUMBER OF PLAYERS: 5+

MATERIALS NEEDED:

- Adhesive nametags for each guest
- Pen or marker

SUMMARY:

Guests create "snapshots" of themselves by drawing pictures on their nametags that reveal something telling about their personalities.

HOW TO PLAY:

1. Party guests are given adhesive name tags upon their arrival, on

which they are instructed to draw or sketch something about themselves. For example, guests who love sports might sketch a tennis racket, the logo of their favorite football team, or a soccer ball. People who enjoy traveling might draw planes and boats, while others might indicate special hobbies or interests.

2. As guests circulate throughout the party, these personalized nametags jump start conversations and help guests learn a little something interesting about others at the party.

VARIATION:

Instead of (or in addition to) pictures, guests may write a word or phrase which best suits their personality. For example, natural jokesters might simply write, "Knock knock" on their nametags—begging the obvious question, "Who's there?"

TIP:

Encourage people to get creative! This is not a contest—just an opportunity to show others a "snapshot" of you!

In every real man a child is hidden that wants to play.

FRIEDRICH NIETZSCHE

Word Games

The versatility and variety of word games makes them well-suited for most any party. Play them when you want to get the party started, or wind things down at the end of an evening.

*I don't give a damn for
a man that can only spell
a word one way.*

MARK TWAIN

CHARADES

The quintessential party game and time-tested favorite for generations!

OBJECTIVE:

To be the fastest team to guess the name of a phrase that your teammates act out.

NUMBER OF PLAYERS: 6+

MATERIALS NEEDED:

- Timer or stopwatch
- Slips of paper
- 2 bowls
- Pens or pencils
- Paper to keep score

SUMMARY:

Players act out a predetermined number of phrases using a series of gestures but no speech. (See "Guide to Gestures for Charades," pages 53-55.) Teams

keep track of how long it takes to figure out the phrases, and the team with the fastest times wins!

HOW TO PLAY:

1. Divide players into two teams of 3+ players each, and instruct teams to think of 5–10 phrases that are titles of books, TV shows, movies, plays, or songs. Teams write down their selected phrases on slips of paper, then fold them and place them into two separate bowls. *Note:* The two teams should agree on phrase categories before they get started.

2. Timed play begins when a player from one team draws a slip of paper from the other team's bowl. This player must act out the phrase to his teammates using a

series of previously agreed upon gestures. Actors may not speak, mouth the words, or point to objects to clue in their teammates. When the team figures out the correct phrase, the timer stops the clock and records the time.

3. Teams play a predetermined number of rounds (3+), alternating turns and making sure all team members have a chance to act out a phrase. The team with the lowest combined overall time wins the game.

Guide to Gestures for Charades

BOOK TITLE:

Open hands with palms upward, as if reading a book.

TELEVISION SHOW:

Use index fingers on each hand to draw a box in the air.

MOVIE:

Look through an imaginary camera by placing one hand by your eye, cupped in an "O" shape, and rotating the other hand as if winding a handle on an old-fashioned movie camera.

PLAY:

Place one hand on your chest and extend the other arm out to the side, as if delivering lines in a play or singing.

SONG:

Open your mouth and pretend to pull out a string of musical notes.

QUOTATION:

Hold up the index and middle fingers on both hands and bend them twice.

NUMBER OF WORDS:

Hold up fingers to indicate the number of words in the phrase.

NUMBER OF SYLLABLES:

Extend your left arm and place fingers from

your right hand on the forearm of your left arm to indicate the number of syllables in the word.

SOUNDS LIKE:

Cup a hand behind your ear, or pull on your ear.

SMALL WORD:

Hold thumb and index finger about an inch apart.

CORRECT ANSWER:

Point your index finger at your nose, as if saying, "You hit it right on the nose!"

VARIATIONS:

1. Instead of teams, individuals take turns drawing slips of paper and acting out phrases to other players.

2. Or, try picture charades (much like the game *Pictionary*), in which players draw pictures of whatever they are trying to convey. In addition to titles, players can decide ahead of time on whatever categories they choose (e.g., proverbs, names of oceans).

TIP:

Choose phrases that contain six words or less that are reasonably easy to decipher.

FORTUNATELY UNFORTUNATELY

Play this game anytime you want to enliven conversation with some creative energy!

OBJECTIVE:

To engage party guests in conversation through creative storytelling.

NUMBER OF PLAYERS: 3+

MATERIALS NEEDED: None

SUMMARY:

An amusing storytelling game in which players take turns making up stories from the point of view of the optimist (*"Fortunately…"*) and the pessimist (*"Unfortunately…"*).

HOW TO PLAY:

1. One person begins telling a story by making up a sentence beginning with the

word "fortunately." For example, "Fortunately for Reuben, Barbara's flight from Costa Rica arrived on time, leaving them two precious hours alone together in the Pie in the Sky airport café."

2. The next player continues the story, but this time starting the sentence with the word "unfortunately." For example, "Unfortunately, Barbara left her prized binoculars on the plane, and spent much of those two hours searching underneath seats and inside overhead compartments to find them."

3. Players alternate telling the tale until it reaches a natural conclusion, and continue the activity as many times as they wish.

Got Game Night?

Why are game nights so popular these days? Find out for yourself by hosting your very own game night!

Party Prep:

Invite at least eight guests over for an evening of fun and games, and make sure you have some tasty snacks and beverages on hand. Wrap up a few fun prize items to make it interesting for your guests. Then, set up three to four game stations or tables with a different board game located at each. Choose from favorites such as *Taboo, Apples to Apples, Cranium,* or *Pictionary,* or design your own combination of board, card, and dice games.

GETTING STARTED:

When your guests arrive, orient them to food, drink, and game stations. Then, group them into teams of three or more players and instruct them to play each game until "time" is called (after about ten minutes or so). Winners of each game should be recorded before teams rotate to different game stations. After teams have rotated through each station, reassemble the players to form different teams, and continue play for as many rounds as desired.

WRAPPING THINGS UP:

At the end of the evening, award prizes to the winners, and perhaps some "honorary" awards to players who made the party especially entertaining or enjoyable.

WORD CON
(a.k.a. *Balderdash*)

Ideal for dinner parties or quiet socializing at the end of an evening.

OBJECTIVE:

To earn the most points by guessing correct answers or convincing other players that your answers are correct.

NUMBER OF PLAYERS: 3+

MATERIALS NEEDED:

- Index Cards
- Pen or pencil
- Dictionary
- Paper to keep score

SUMMARY:

Players randomly select index cards containing unusual vocabulary words and give definitions of these words to other players, even if they have to make them up. Players earn points for correctly guessing whether the definitions provided are "true" or "false," and by convincing other players that their definitions are correct.

HOW TO PLAY:

1. Before the party, the host finds 15+ unusual or obscure words in the dictionary, and writes them on index cards. (See "Sample Words," page 62.)

2. To begin the game, a player (the "word con") chooses an index card containing one vocabulary word, and provides a definition of that word to the other players. For example, if the word is *expectorate*, the player might make up a definition (e.g., to state one's expectations in a preachy or didactic manner), or provide the correct definition, if known (e.g., to spit).

3. Each player considers the definition provided and states whether he believes it

 is "true" or "false." Once everyone has answered, the "word con" reads aloud the correct definition as it appears in the dictionary. Players earn one point each for their correct answers, and the "word con" earns one point for each player who believes his correct definition was false or his made-up definition was correct.

4. After everyone has had the opportunity to be the "word con," the player with the most points wins!

Sample Words

Aspic	*Oleaginous*
Cynosure	*Quisling*
Formic	*Sapient*
Fustian	*Stentorian*
Miasma	*Viviparous*

1. Instead of using index cards, players select a random word from the dictionary and either read its definition or fabricate their own.

2. Rules can allow the word con to use either a real or made-up word. If the word con makes up a non-existent word with a (by definition, phony) definition, players who guess that the word does not exist score one point. The word con scores a point for each player who believes it is a real word.

TIP:

When compiling words for the game, be sure to include some words that your guests might actually know.

THE LAST WORD

Enjoy this game while socializing around the dinner table, or anytime you wish to spark creative conversation.

OBJECTIVE:

To engage party guests in conversation through creative storytelling.

NUMBER OF PLAYERS: 3+

MATERIALS NEEDED: None

SUMMARY:

A creative storytelling game in which each player makes up a portion of a story, and the next player must start his part of the story using the last word spoken by the previous storyteller.

HOW TO PLAY:

1. One player begins the game by making up the first sentence of a story (e.g.,

James Patrick couldn't believe his ears when he was named, "Man of the Year.")

2. The next player continues the story by starting with the last word of the previous sentence (e.g., *Year after year, James heard the names of neighbors, friends, and scoundrels, never expecting to read his name on a plaque at Town Hall.*)

3. The next person continues the story with a sentence beginning with the word "hall," and so on. Players continue taking turns telling the story for as long as desired, being sure to begin with the last word of the previous sentence.

TIP:

Make your story uniquely entertaining by adding weird or creative twists, or incorporating the names of people at your party!

BLURT
(a.k.a. *Outburst*)

A high energy game that requires quick thinking and a quicker tongue!

OBJECTIVE:

To blurt out the most correct answers within a given timeframe.

NUMBER OF PLAYERS: 6+

MATERIALS NEEDED:

- Slips of paper
- Bowl
- Paper to keep score
- Pens or pencils
- Timer or stopwatch

SUMMARY:

Teams blurt out as many correct answers as possible to a series of questions within a given timeframe. The team with the highest number of correct answers wins!

HOW TO PLAY:

1. Before the party, the host writes down 10–15 topics or categories on slips of paper, then folds them and puts them in a bowl. (See "Sample Categories," on page 68.)

2. To play, guests are divided into two teams. Each team takes turns drawing categories from the bowl, and players have 60 seconds to blurt out as many things as come to mind relating to that topic. For example, if the topic is "pasta," team members will blurt out as many different kinds of pasta as they can think of (e.g., spaghetti, ziti, macaroni).

3. Teams take turns timing each other and drawing categories from the bowl. After an equal number of turns, teams tally up their correct answers, and the team with the highest number wins!

Sample Categories

Ice cream flavors	*Varieties of flowers*
Male names beginning with the letter "n"	*Foreign languages*
	Sports involving a ball
Cartoon characters	

VARIATIONS:

1. For individual play, all players require pen and paper with which to record their answers. The host, or another designated player, draws a category and reads it aloud. Players have 60 seconds to write down as many answers as possible. When time is up, the player with the most correct answers wins.

2. Instead of the host, all the players can brainstorm for categories before the game. For added difficulty, players may choose three answers for each category that *will not count* toward the final score. For example, if the category is "pasta,"

the opposing team may identify three types of pasta that do not count (e.g., spaghetti, ziti, macaroni). This requires the team to brainstorm  for less obvious answers (e.g., orzo, rigatoni, lasagna). You may also wish to deduct a point for each wrong answer.

3. Instead of categories, players take turns reading a random definition from the dictionary, and the other players try to figure out the word to which the definition applies. The first player to blurt out the correct word wins!

> *The game* Scrabble *is found in one out of every three American homes.*

In the Manner of the Adverb

Hilarious improvisation game!

Objective:

To guess the adverb that describes the manner in which a scene is improvised in the shortest amount of time.

Number of Players: 4+

Materials Needed:

- Timer or stopwatch
- Paper to record time
- Pen or pencil

Summary:

The player designated as "It" has two minutes or less to identify the adverb that best describes *how* other players respond to his questions.

How to Play:

1. The player designated as "It" leaves the

room while the rest of the players think of an adverb (e.g., lovingly, cruelly, impatiently). See other sample adverbs on page 72.

2. After "It" returns to the room, the clock starts when he asks various open-ended questions of each player (e.g., What is your favorite type of music/food/drink? How did you meet the host/your spouse/etc.? Who is your favorite athlete/movie star/etc.?).

3. Players must attempt to respond to these questions "in the manner of the adverb." For example, if the adverb chosen is "impatiently," each player will try to act in an impatient manner when answering the questions. Responses might be hurried, and mannerisms could include tapping feet, snapping fingers, and exasperated breaths.

4. "It" must figure out the adverb within two minutes or less. If so, his time is recorded and another person takes a turn as "It." If not, his time is recorded as two minutes, and another person becomes "It." After all players have taken a turn as "It," the player with the fastest time wins!

Sample Adverbs	
Abruptly	*Lethargically*
Cantankerously	*Mischievously*
Eagerly	*Offensively*
Gregariously	*Slowly*
Icily	*Weakly*

VARIATION:

Instead of questions, players draw from two bowls: one that contains folded slips of paper with adverbs; and the other with folded slips of paper on which speech topics are written. Examples of speech topics could be: *How to Survive the Holidays* or *The Most*

Important Lessons I Learned in High School. "It" draws from the adverb bowl, and he must deliver whatever speech topic is drawn by someone else "in the manner of the adverb." The first person to guess the adverb wins the round.

It is a happy talent to know how to play.

RALPH WALDO EMERSON

Physical Games

Physical games involve some degree of movement, and therefore may not be suited to certain indoor parties or parties in which the age, dress, or physical ability of guests prohibits them from participating. But at outdoor parties or roomy, indoor facilities, physical games—or games that require people to work in teams to accomplish physical tasks—can be a great way to bring people together in a spirit of fun.

You can discover more about a person in an hour of play than in a year of conversation.

PLATO

BACK TO BACK

Amusing and challenging game
requiring dexterity and teamwork!

OBJECTIVE:

For partners to gently place a hard-boiled
egg on the ground using only their backs.

NUMBER OF PLAYERS: 4+

MATERIALS NEEDED:

2+ eggs (enough for each pair of players
and subsequent rounds)

SUMMARY:

Standing back to back, teams of partners
attempt to carefully move an egg from
between their shoulder blades to the ground
below without breaking it. The first team to
succeed wins!

HOW TO PLAY:

1. Players split up into pairs, and each pair
   receives one egg. Players are instructed to

stand back to back and place the egg between their upper shoulder blades.

2. Upon hearing the word "Go," players use only their backs (no hands!) in an attempt to move the egg to the ground *without breaking it.* The first pair to succeed wins the game!

VARIATIONS:

1. Instead of back to back, players can play subsequent rounds in other compromising positions—side to side or front to front.

2. Instead of hard-boiled eggs, use water balloons, balls, fruits, or vegetables.

3. Instead of moving an object from high to low, try the reverse! Standing face to face, partners can roll an object from their belly buttons to their chins.

BOUNTY HUNTER

(a.k.a. Scavenger Hunt)

Great activity for guests while host prepares food or cleans up!

OBJECTIVE:

To find and seize hidden bounty items.

NUMBER OF PLAYERS: 6+ (at least 2 teams of 3 players each)

MATERIALS NEEDED:

- Paper for lists
- Pen or pencil

SUMMARY:

Teams have 30 minutes to search a designated area on the party premises to find the bounty items on their lists. The first team to seize their bounty wins!

HOW TO PLAY:

1. Before the party, the host writes down two lists, each containing the same five

bounty items (see below). These items should be everyday things that individuals might carry with them (e.g., in a wallet, a car, or a pocket), or those that can be found outside (e.g., a yellow flower, a pebble).

2. To play, guests are divided into two teams and given a list of items they need to find within 30 minutes. At the host's discretion, guests may ask any non-participating guests for assistance, or may be permitted to search a designated area on the party premises. The first team to collect the items on its list wins a prize!

Sample Bounty Items

Receipt with today's date	A Band-Aid
A live insect	Coin dated within five years of today's date
Photograph of a baby	A coupon

For adventurous types, instead of playing this game at the party, give guests exactly one hour to leave the party and search for the bounty items on their list. This variation allows for greater flexibility in both the number and types of bounty items you include (e.g., photo of someone with a tattoo, autograph of someone named John), and works best in city neighborhood where guests don't need to roam far.

SAFETY TIP:

Don't encourage guests to drive vehicles in search of bounty if they have been drinking alcohol!

FOX AND SQUIRREL

Fast, frenetic fun for everyone!

OBJECTIVE:
To "catch the squirrel" by tagging whoever is holding the squirrel ball with one or both of the fox balls.

NUMBER OF PLAYERS: 6+

MATERIALS NEEDED:
Three balls (2 large, 1 small)

SUMMARY:
Players form a circle and are given three balls: two larger balls for the "foxes," and one smaller ball for the "squirrel." The foxes attempt to catch the squirrel by passing the larger balls from person to person and tagging the person with the squirrel ball. The squirrel avoids being caught by throwing the smaller ball across the circle to another player.

HOW TO PLAY:

1. Players stand in a circle and are given three balls: two larger balls for the foxes, and one smaller ball for the squirrel. Fox balls must be passed from one person to another, while the squirrel ball may be either passed or thrown across the circle. (Squirrels can jump, after all!)

2. Play begins when fox and squirrel balls are passed between players. Each time a player receives a ball, he must yell "Fox!" or "Squirrel!" depending on which ball he is holding. Players attempt to tag the person holding the squirrel ball with one or both fox balls. The faster the pace of play, the better the chance to out-fox the squirrel!

KNOTS

Great team-building activity!

OBJECTIVE:

To untangle a human knot without releasing hands.

NUMBER OF PLAYERS: 6+

MATERIALS NEEDED: None

SUMMARY:

Players form a human knot and must figure out how to untangle it without releasing their hands.

HOW TO PLAY:

1. Players form a circle. Each person extends his right hand into the center of the circle and clasps the right hand of a person *not* standing next to him. Players then extend their left hands into the center of the circle and clasp the left hand of a different player *not* standing

next to them.

2. Without releasing hands, players must figure out how to untangle their knot!

TIP:

Untangled knots may resemble the number eight.

LOOP THE HOOP

Good, clean, hoopy fun!

OBJECTIVE:

To pass a hula hoop around a circle while holding hands.

NUMBER OF PLAYERS: 8+

MATERIALS NEEDED:

One large hula hoop

SUMMARY:

Players challenge themselves to pass a hula hoop around a circle without releasing their hands.

HOW TO PLAY:

Players form a big circle and hold hands. One pair lets go for just a moment to allow a hula hoop to encircle their joined hands. Players maneuver their bodies in order to pass the hula hoop from one person to another, until it goes full circle.

1. Make the task more challenging by adding rules or requirements (e.g., Players must stand on one foot).

2. Add a second hoop and keep two hoops moving around the circle at the same time.

GREAT OUTDOOR GAMES

Thinking of throwing a backyard brouhaha? Graduation party? Family reunion? Before you fire up the grill, consider these classic outdoor games and their infinite variations to really get your party cooking!

CLASSIC GAME: CROQUET
Variations:

- Obstacle Course Croquet: Add unexpected obstacles or challenges to the croquet course, including water features, hills and valleys, and detours.

- Golf Croquet: Use golf clubs to hit golf balls through croquet wickets.

CLASSIC GAME: BADMINTON
Variation:

- Really Badminton: Players must use their non-dominant hands to play traditional badminton.

CLASSIC GAME: VOLLEYBALL
Variations:

- Beach Volleyball: Use a beach ball instead of a traditional volleyball.

- Balloon Volleyball: Use balloons instead of a traditional volleyball.

- Blind Beach Volleyball: Obstruct players' views of the other side of the net using a sheet or tarp to add an element of surprise to the game.

CLASSIC GAME: HORSESHOES
Variation:

- Target Practice: Instead of horseshoes, make a game of tossing plastic rings, Frisbees, or balls at different targets.

CLASSIC GAME: EGG TOSS
Variation:

- Catch or Else: Instead of eggs, players play catch with water balloons or other potentially messy items (e.g., tomatoes), taking one large step back between throws until only one pair remains.

CLASSIC GAME: BOCCE BALL
Variation:

- Bocce Bowl: Set up various objects to serve as "pins," and roll bocce balls to knock them down, as if bowling.

CLASSIC GAME: RELAY RACES
Variation:

- Fear Factor Medley: Depending on how game your guests are, you might consider adding new challenges to a variety of traditional relay races to *really* up the stakes! Try any combination of the following games for teams of two: Blind Obstacle Relay; Two-legged Sack Race; Greased Cucumber Relay; or Blind Piggy Back Relay.

Silly Games

Games designed for the sole purpose of making people laugh may be termed "silly," but try them at your next party and you and your guests will be laughing till it hurts.

We're fools whether
we dance or not, so we
might as well dance.

JAPANESE PROVERB

TOP MODEL
(a.k.a. Funny Face Contest)

Only for people with a sensc of humor!

OBJECTIVE:

To win the honors of "Top Model" by achieving the most unique and contorted facial expression.

NUMBER OF PLAYERS: 3+

MATERIALS NEEDED:

- Slips of Paper
- Pens and pencils

SUMMARY:

Guests contort their faces in unique and creative ways in order to be judged "Top Model."

HOW TO PLAY:

1. The host announces a casting call for models,

and explains that the model who exhibits the most creative and unique "look" wins a prize.

2. One at a time, potential models strike poses for the crowd, and after the final candidate, partygoers write their pick for Top Model on a slip of paper.

3. The winner is recognized and awarded a prize.

VARIATION:

Use a digital or Polaroid camera to snap photos of models and display them for judging by party guests.

TIP:

Add to the drama by awarding the winner a

 long-stemmed red rose, a sash featuring the words "Top Model," or a crown.

CHICKEN

Never fails to amuse!

OBJECTIVE:
To make people laugh.

NUMBER OF PLAYERS: 5+

MATERIALS NEEDED:
A rubber chicken

SUMMARY:

The person designated as "It" sits in the center of a circle and interacts with a rubber chicken in a manner designed to elicit laughter from the other participants. The first person to laugh becomes "It."

HOW TO PLAY:

The host instructs partygoers to form a circle (or reasonable facsimile thereof) so that they can discuss something very serious: the game known as "Chicken." To play, the person designated as "It" sits in the center of the circle and improvises with a rubber chicken. For example, "It" might engage in imaginary conversation with the chicken (e.g., *Why won't you answer me, chicken?*) or hold its rubbery body in such a way as to provoke laughter from others. Whoever laughs first becomes "It."

VARIATION:

In the absence of a rubber chicken, the host may consider using another stuffed or plastic creature. But be warned: nothing beats a rubber chicken.

ICE DANCER

Great way to liven up the dance floor!

OBJECTIVE:

To sport the most unique and admirable dance moves from the waist up.

NUMBER OF PLAYERS: 3+

MATERIALS NEEDED:
Music

SUMMARY:

Contestants participate in a dance-off in which they are "frozen" from the waist down. The person with the most unique and admirable dance moves wins!

HOW TO PLAY:

1. The host gets the attention of party guests by announcing that an "ice" dancing competition will take place on the dance floor (or

wherever), and they have five minutes to practice their dance moves while "frozen" from the waist down. The host also asks for two volunteers to assist in the judging process.

2. When the competition begins, guests exhibit all their very best dance moves using only their arms, shoulders, necks, and heads. Dancers must otherwise remain "frozen" from the waist down, and those who move body parts below the waist will be disqualified (allow one or two warnings). The dancer with the best moves wins!

VARIATIONS:

1. There are many hilarious variations to this game, in which dancers must challenge themselves to conform to different rules or restrictions about how and when to dance. For example, instead of being frozen from

the waist down, dancers may be told to "freeze" one or more body parts (e.g., shoulders, buttocks) at different times of a song.

2. Try "role play" dance moves. For example, dance as if you are in the process of doing something else. To "mow the lawn," for example, strut to the beat with an imaginary lawnmower. The possibilities are endless, and your guests will have infinite fun creating their own special variations to favorites such as the "wash the car" and "walk the dog."

TIP:

Introduce silly dancing games to lure reluctant dancers onto the dance floor, or just for some lighthearted fun. The sillier the moves, the less self-conscious dancers will feel.

BANANA PONG

Golf for the equipment challenged!

OBJECTIVE:

To be the first player to roll a Ping-Pong ball across the finish line.

NUMBER OF PLAYERS: 4+

MATERIALS NEEDED:
- Bananas for each player
- Ping-Pong balls for each player
- String, yarn, or twine
- Scissors
- Tape

SUMMARY:

Players race to move a Ping-Pong ball to the finish line using only a banana hung from their wrists.

HOW TO PLAY:

1. Each player is given a banana, a Ping-Pong ball, and a length of string, and

instructed to tie one end of the string to the banana, and the other end to their wrists. It might be a good idea to use a piece of tape to reinforce the string to the banana.

2. Players line up at the starting line and place their Ping-Pong balls at their feet. At the word, "Go," they must swing their arms in an effort to whack the Ping-Pong ball with the banana. The first player to get their Ping-Pong ball across the finish line wins!

VARIATIONS:

1. Instead of wrists, hang bananas from strings attached to players' waists, or clutched in their teeth.

2. Vary both the ball and the instrument with which to hit the ball. For example, instead of Ping-Pong balls, use

Wiffle balls or beach balls. Instead of bananas, try vegetables such as zucchini or corn on the cob, or any other object that can suit the purpose.

TIP:
Put initials on balls or mark them in some way to keep straight whose is whose.

In 1983, the game Monopoly was played for a record 1,080 hours underwater. Some 350 members of the Buffalo Dive Club took turns using a special laminated Monopoly set over a span of 45 days.

Balloon Head

Provides take-home favors for your guests!

Objective:

To match the face on the balloon with the guest.

Number of Players: 6+

Materials Needed:

- 6+ balloons
- Permanent markers for each guest

Summary:

Participants attempt to draw portraits of their partners on inflated balloons, and guests must try to match the balloon with the correct person.

How to Play:

1. The host inflates enough balloons for everyone at the party, and gives each guest a balloon and permanent marker. Players are organized into pairs and

instructed to draw a portrait of their partner on the balloon.

2. After all the balloon portraits have been completed, balloons are bunched together and mixed up, and players must try to match the balloon portrait with the correct person.

VARIATION:

Have a contest to judge the best balloon portrait artist!

Mystery Games

Who doesn't love a good mystery? Whether it's a missing diamond tiara or a murder in the study, your guests will enjoy playing detective and villain every step of the way.

Elementary, my dear Watson!

WINK

(a.k.a. Assassin or Murder)

Great for cocktail parties and *murderous* mixers!

OBJECTIVE:

To figure out the identity of the "assassin" who "murders" his victims by winking at them.

NUMBER OF PLAYERS: 5+

MATERIALS NEEDED:

- Slips of folded paper for each guest
- Bowl

SUMMARY:

A designated assassin inconspicuously winks at different party guests, "killing" them off one by one until someone figures out his true identity.

HOW TO PLAY:

1. Players draw slips of folded paper from a

bowl, in which one slip contains an "X." The player who draws the "X" becomes the assassin, and he proceeds to eliminate other players from the  game by winking at them as inconspicuously as possible. In order to protect the identity of the assassin, victims should wait a few seconds before crying out, swooning, and dying as dramatically as possible. Players who have been eliminated leave the game.

2. When a player thinks he can identify the assassin, he points to the person and says, "I accuse you." If he is wrong, he dies. But if he is correct, he wins the round, and the game can start again.

VARIATION:

Mark two slips of paper, one with an "X" for the assassin and another with a "D" for the detective. After drawing slips of paper, the detective announces his identity and leaves the room. If possible, the lights in the room are turned off while the detective is out of the room. The assassin kills one victim by gently tapping him on the shoulder, and the victim screams and collapses dead to the floor. The lights are then turned back on and the players call the detective. The detective asks questions to figure out the assassin's identity, but the players do not have to tell the truth. The detective gets three guesses to solve the mystery. (You'll be surprised how often the assassin acts "guilty" and can be guessed.)

RED-HANDED

How good is your poker face?

OBJECTIVE:

To inconspicuously pass an object around a circle and avoid being caught "red-handed" holding the object.

NUMBER OF PLAYERS: 6+

MATERIALS NEEDED:

A marble or other small object

SUMMARY:

While the person designated as "It" stands in the center of the circle, players make a series of actual and fake hand-to-hand passes of an object. "It" must determine which player is holding the object, and catch him "red-handed."

HOW TO PLAY:

1. Players stand in a circle, and the person designated as "It"

stands in the center of the circle.

2. While "It" closes his eyes, the players either pass the object from one person to another, or pretend to pass the object.

3. When "It" signals and opens his eyes, he must determine which player is holding the object. He approaches the players who appear guilty and tap their fists to reveal their contents. Meanwhile, other players with or without the object continue to make a series of actual and fake passes to further confuse "It."

4. The player caught red-handed holding the object becomes "It."

TIP:

Hold the object in one hand, palm down, and drop it into the palm-up hand of the next person. The sneakier the better!

CRIME SCENE

Play this game throughout the course of an evening, or as an after-dinner activity for guests with playful spirits and clever minds!

OBJECTIVE:

To unravel a mysterious crime scene by figuring out riddles and finding hidden clues.

NUMBER OF PLAYERS: 6+

MATERIALS NEEDED:

- Paper for clues and riddles
- Pens or pencils

SUMMARY:

Players try to solve a murder mystery by figuring out riddles and finding hidden clues at the crime scene.

HOW TO PLAY:

1. The host draws up a

series of riddles in which the answers lead to clues hidden somewhere at the party. For example, the host might write, "I am there for you in your darkest hours" on a piece of paper. Players brainstorm for answers (e.g., flashlight? matches? candle?), and look for clues near or around these items.

2. When players solve the first riddle ("It's a lamp!"), they will find yet another clue (in this case, under the lamp) in the form of a riddle. The host may leave as many clues as desired, ultimately leading players to a final clue which will allow them to solve the mystery. The first player(s) to correctly identify the murderer and the murder weapon wins!

VARIATIONS:

1. Instead of a murder mystery, keep the spirit of your mystery lighthearted. Why not have guests solve mysteries about missing objects, such as paintings or

jewels or the pooch?

2. Or, have clues ultimately lead to a table of food, or a prize to be shared!

TIP:

Make up riddles about everyday items (e.g., vase, umbrella, hat) found in the area designated for the party, or about unusual or unique household fixtures or knickknacks.

DINNER PARTY WHODUNITS

Hosting a dinner party mystery is easier than you might think! Check out your local bookstore or game retailer for off-the-shelf mystery game kits, or just type "murder mystery" into your browser and view infinite online options that you can purchase and download. Here are a few sites to get you started:

murdermysterygames.com

mysteriesonthenet.com

murdermysterygame.com

Drinking Games

As people have known for thousands of years, the addition of alcohol in any game—whether as a prop, a penalty, or a prize—makes for a whole lotta fun. But even if you're drinking sparkling water or a tall glass of milk, you can't help but enjoy playing these inventive and revealing games.

Health—what my friends
are always drinking to before
they fall down.

PHYLLIS DILLER

ZOOM, SCHWARTZ, PIFIGLIANO

 Hilarious drinking game that is not as easy at it sounds!

OBJECTIVE:

To be the last remaining player in this rapid-fire concentration game.

NUMBER OF PLAYERS: 4+

MATERIALS NEEDED:

Your favorite alcoholic beverage

SUMMARY:

Players attempt to communicate in a particular order using only eye contact (or the lack thereof), and the words "zoom," "schwartz," and "pifigliano."

HOW TO PLAY:

1. Players sit in a circle or around a table. The game begins when a person looks at

someone else and says, "Zoom." This is called "zooming" and you always look at the person you are zooming.

2. The person who has been zoomed may then look at someone else and say "Zoom," or get the first person back by saying, "Schwartz," *but without looking at that person*.

3. If the first person has been schwartzed, he can either look at a new person and say "Zoom," or send it right back to the second person by saying "Pifigliano" — again *without looking at that person*.

4. The game continues until someone breaks the rules by looking at the wrong person when they speak, or speaking out of order. Whoever makes a mistake must take a drink, and players are disqualified from the game after three mistakes.

TIP:

Choose your own silly words or names.

THUMPER

Classic drinking game that's practically a rite of passage!

OBJECTIVE:

To be the last remaining player in this fast-paced coordination and concentration game.

NUMBER OF PLAYERS: 5+

MATERIALS NEEDED:

Your favorite alcoholic beverage

SUMMARY:

A gesture game in which participants thump their legs in sync while chanting the Thumper refrain ("What's the name of the game?..."), and imitate each other's quirky signals.

HOW TO PLAY:

1. Each player adopts a personal signal or combination of signals, such as flapping arms, giving the peace sign, or winking

while giving the thumbs up.

2. To play, everyone sits in a circle and alternately slaps their thighs. One player says, "What's the name of the game?" In unison, the rest of the players answer, "Thumper." The first player continues, "How do you play it?" and the others answer, "All the way!" Players then take turns going around the circle gesturing their signals to show other players what they are.

3. Play officially begins when the first player gestures his signal and follows it with someone else's signal. The person whose signal has been displayed must then gesture his own signal and follow it with another player's signal. Play continues until someone makes a mistake, at which point he must take a drink. Players are disqualified from the

game after three mistakes. That is, if anybody's counting.

Note: Feel free to say the refrain—"What's the name of the game?"—every time someone has to take a drink.

*We are most nearly ourselves
when we achieve the seriousness
of the child at play.*

HERACLITUS

NEVER HAVE I EVER

Great way to expose a few skeletons in the closet!

OBJECTIVE:

To learn a few intriguing details about your friends, and reveal a few shockers of your own!

NUMBER OF PLAYERS: 3+

MATERIALS NEEDED:

Your favorite alcoholic beverage

SUMMARY:

Players take turns making a statement that begins with the phrase, "Never have I ever…" and anyone who *can not* agree with the statement takes a drink.

HOW TO PLAY:

1. The first player begins the game by making a statement that begins with the phrase, "Never have I ever…" For example, "Never have I ever gotten a

body piercing." Whoever has gotten a body piercing must take a drink.

2. Statements start out benign, but in time beg for more intimate revelations— "Never have I ever gotten a tattoo below the navel," "Never have I ever posed for a nude photograph," and so on. The game may become quite confessional, as people are inspired to go into details to explain any particularly intimate or revealing details. Or, they can simply raise their glass and take a drink. In this game, actions speak louder than words!

TIP:

Alcohol serves as a truth serum in this game.

QUARTERS

A classic drinking game that never goes out of style!

OBJECTIVE:

To bounce a coin off a table and into a shot glass.

NUMBER OF PLAYERS: 3+

MATERIALS NEEDED:

- Beer
- Shot glass
- A quarter or other coin
- Table or other hard surface

SUMMARY:

Players attempt to bounce a quarter off a table so that it lands inside a shot glass. When it does, the shooter either chooses someone to take a drink or—if he sinks three quarters in a row—makes up a new rule.

HOW TO PLAY:

1. Players stand in a circle around a table and spin a quarter. Whoever the nose (or beak) points toward goes first.

2. The first player bounces the quarter off the table in an attempt to make it land inside the shot glass. If successful, the shooter gets to pick someone to take a drink. A quarter that hits the glass but does not go in warrants another try. A shooter plays until he completely misses the glass, at which point he passes the quarter to the person standing to his left.

3. If any shooter gets three quarters inside the glass in a row, he gets to make up a rule (e.g., No beer in the right hand, No use of anyone's first name, etc.).

VARIATIONS:

1. If players get too proficient at bouncing quarters the usual way, up the stakes by requiring

them to bounce quarters with their non-dominant hands, or by rolling them off elbows and noses!

2. Instead of coins, try bouncing Ping-Pong balls into cups or glasses filled with beer. Whoever gets the ball inside the glass gets to choose someone to take a drink!

THE NAME GAME

The more you think, the more you drink!

OBJECTIVE:

To think of names within a certain category as quickly as possible.

NUMBER OF PLAYERS: 3+

MATERIALS NEEDED:

Your favorite alcoholic beverage

SUMMARY:

A fast-paced word game in which players must think of names within a certain category, and drink while they think!

HOW TO PLAY:

1. Players choose or make up any category of people—actors, singers, people you want to see naked, and so on. The first player begins the game by calling out the

first and last name of any individual who falls into the designated category. For example, if the category is "actors," he might say "Brad Pitt."

2. The next player notes the first letter of the last name called (P in Pitt) and responds by calling out the name of an actor whose first name starts with the same letter (e.g., Penélope Cruz). Players must *drink* while they *think*, so they should try to think fast!

3. The next player must come up with an actor whose first name begins with C (e.g., Colin Farrell), and so on. When a name with double initials is called (e.g., Ozzie Osbourne, Sharon Stone), then the order of the circle reverses to counterclockwise.

4. Play continues until the category is exhausted, then starts again with a new category.

Fuzzy Duck

A true tongue-tripper!

Objective:

To repeat the words "fuzzy duck," "ducky fuzz," or "does he" in the right order without making a mistake.

Number of Players: 4+

Materials Needed:

Your favorite alcoholic beverage.

Summary:

Players go around the room repeating the words "fuzzy duck," "does he (duzzy)," or "ducky fuzz" in order, and whoever makes a mistake must take a drink.

How to Play:

1. One player begins the game by saying "fuzzy duck," and the player to his left must repeat the words "fuzzy duck" to the player on his left, and so on.

2. To change the direction and the phrase, a player can say, "Does he? (duzzy)" and the player on his right must say "ducky fuzz" to the player on his right, and so on. Players must take a drink whenever they make a mistake.

VARIATION:

Make up new rules for each round, such as requiring players to say something different each time it is their turn. For example, if a player says "fuzzy duck" the first time, then he must say something else (e.g., "does he" or "ducky fuzz") the next time.

TIP:

Add to the confusion by looking at the wrong player when saying your phrase (e.g., looking to the right, not the left, when you say "fuzzy duck").

BOXHEAD

Lotsa fun! Lotsa drinking!

OBJECTIVE:
To get lucky while rolling the dice.

NUMBER OF PLAYERS: 6+

MATERIALS NEEDED:
- Pair of dice
- Shot glass
- Penalty drink (hard liquor)
- Beer
- Box (e.g., a 6-pack or 12-pack beer box)

SUMMARY:
Players take turns rolling dice and following rules assigned to dice totals (see next page).

HOW TO PLAY:
Players sit around a table and take turns rolling the dice, then adhere to pre-determined rules that apply to dice totals.

Dice Totals:

2: Double Odds (see page 130).

3: Person to the left of the roller drinks.

4: No action required (unless it's two 2's—see Double Evens, page 130).

5: Roll one die to determine how many drinks each player must take.

6: Create or change a rule (and if it's two 3's—see Double Odds, page 130).

7: Everyone must put their thumbs on the table, and the last person must drink.

8: Penalty shot. Roll one die to determine how much the shot glass is filled. 1–3=half shot; 4–6=full shot.

9: Person to the right of the roller drinks.

10: Bathroom break. No one leaves the table until they roll a 10 (unless it's two 5's—see Double Odds, page 130).

11: Boxhead (see page 130).

12: Boxhead (see below, unless it's two 6's—see Double Evens below).

Double Evens (e.g., two 2's, 4's, 6's)
Roller drinks (in addition to any other applicable rules).

Double Odds (e.g., two 1's, 3's, 5's)
Everybody drinks (in addition to any other applicable rules).

Boxhead
Whoever rolls an 11 or 12 must wear a box on their head until someone else rolls another 11 or 12. The boxhead must drink whenever someone else drinks, except for the penalty shot.

VARIATION:
Decide as a group the rules and penalties for dice totals, and vary them with each round played.

TIP:

If the game lasts longer than anticipated, substitute beer or a nonalcoholic beverage for hard liquor on penalty shots.

Some of the first games, such as chess, checkers, and playing cards, were "war" games representing army formations and military strategies.

Naughty Games

Naughty games can be oh so good, especially when you're in mixed company and feeling a little randy. Is it getting hot in here?

Sex appeal is 50% what you've got and 50% what people think you've got.

SOPHIA LOREN

ORANGE APPEAL

Great way to bring your guests face to face!

OBJECTIVE:

To successfully pass an orange from person to person using only their necks.

NUMBER OF PLAYERS: 6+

MATERIALS NEEDED:

Orange

SUMMARY:

Participants must pass an orange from person to person using only their necks.

HOW TO PLAY:

1. Players are instructed to stand in a circle. One player starts the game by placing an orange underneath her neck, and attempting to pass the orange to the player to her right using only

her neck and chin (no hands!). Players who drop the orange are disqualified.

2. After the orange makes it around the circle once, the first player makes up a new rule (e.g., players must stand on one foot only, players must maintain eye contact while they pass the orange). The next time the orange makes it around the circle, the second player makes up a rule. Play continues until only two people remain standing.

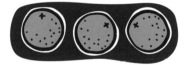

ACRONYMPHOMANIAC

No word is safe in this naughty little game!

OBJECTIVE:

To make up suggestive acronym definitions for random words.

NUMBER OF PLAYERS: 3+

MATERIALS NEEDED: None

SUMMARY:

Players use their imaginations to create sexually suggestive acronym definitions for random words.

HOW TO PLAY:

Players select words, then brainstorm together to create acronym definitions using each letter of the word. For example, if the word is "Kiss," players think of words or phrases beginning with each letter of the word "kiss": Kinky Invigorating Succulent

Smooch; or Know-how In Swapping Spit.

TIP:

Choose innocent, everyday words (e.g., soap, mailman, tuna), or spice up some already suggestive words or slang (e.g., grind, pimp). Your acronym definitions will say it all!

DIRTY MINDS

Great way to plant naughty thoughts in the most innocent of ways!

OBJECTIVE:

To figure out simple riddles that double as sexual innuendos.

NUMBER OF PLAYERS: 3+

MATERIALS NEEDED:

- Paper for each player
- Pens or pencils

SUMMARY:

Players make up sexually suggestive clues or riddles about ordinary objects, and other players attempt to solve them.

HOW TO PLAY:

1. Each player is given a piece of paper and a pen or pencil, and instructed to write a sexually suggestive riddle about

 an ordinary object (e.g., paper, peanut butter) in an attempt to confuse (and perhaps titillate?) other players. For example, if the object is paper, possible riddles might be: *Sometimes I'm flat, other times I'm stacked; I come in sheets.* Clues for peanut butter might include: *I can leave you speechless; spread me before you eat me.*

2. When people blush or gasp in horror at a particular riddle, their dirty minds have clearly been exposed! (These are normal, everyday objects, after all.) Players take turns reading their riddles while others attempt to solve them, and whoever solves the most riddles wins.

VARIATION:

For larger groups (or even more fun), try to stump other players by working in teams of two or more.

If you don't want to make up your own riddles, go out and buy the game *Dirty Minds*!

*It is in games that many
men discover their paradise.*

ROBERT LYND

Daring Hearts

This game is sure to get hearts beating!

Objective:

To get people to reveal personal truths to probing questions, and perform challenging dares.

Number of Players: 4+

Materials Needed:

- Deck of playing cards
- Alcoholic beverage of choice

Summary:

Players take turns flipping over playing cards, and must drink, answer questions, and/or perform dares whenever hearts come up.

How to Play:

1. Players sit in a circle and take turns flipping over one playing card at a time from a deck of cards.

2. Whenever a person flips over a heart card with a face value between 2 and 10, other players ask him a question. The person chooses one question to  answer, and the players whose questions have not been selected must take a drink.

Note: If the selected heart card is a jack, queen, king, or ace, then each player asks a question and proposes a dare. The person chooses two questions to answer and one dare. Players whose questions and/or dares have not been selected must take a drink.

VARIATION:

Instead of drinking alcohol, players can draw from a bowl with various dares or questions that they must perform or answer.

HOT LIPS

(a.k.a. Pin the __ on the __)

A kissing game that's full of surprises!

OBJECTIVE:

To plant a kiss in the right place.

NUMBER OF PLAYERS: 5+

MATERIALS NEEDED:

- Colorful lipstick or lip gloss
- Large picture or illustration of a person
- Tape
- Blindfold

SUMMARY:

A naughty version of the classic game, "Pin the Tail on the Donkey," in which players attempt to make a kiss mark closest to a designated target area (lips?) while wearing a blindfold and lipstick.

HOW TO PLAY:

1. Before the party, the host finds or draws a

poster-sized picture of a person and tapes it to a wall about three feet off the ground. This picture may be a photographic image, a cartoon caricature, or a simple illustration.

2. To play, participants stand about ten feet from the wall and prime their lips with colorful lipstick (the guys will just love this!). Each player takes a turn wearing a blindfold, walking toward the wall, and attempting to make a kiss mark on a designated target area. The player who comes closest to the target area wins a prize!

VARIATION:

Instead of lipstick, players can use stickers to leave their mark on the picture.

TIP:

Have one person spin the blindfolded player around three times before they're directed toward the wall.

INDEX OF GAMES